HOW TO BECOME A FASHION DESIGNER

NADJA SOLOVIEVA

Published by Vieva Books 2025
Edited by Alexander Atwater

Introduction

To be a Fashion Designer is a desirable profession which can be widely stereotyped or idealised. We have created this book as a simple and comprehensive introductory guide on how to approach this career path, and the education required.

Fashion is more than a skill to dress people. Fashion can influence the world. This power comes with even more responsibility, considering important factors such as ecology and sustainability.

Fashion makes our lives more beautiful, comfortable, and joyful every day. It is able to keep us warm, uplift our mood, and make us feel comfortable and self-expressed, thanks to everyone in this industry.

"You have to have a complete understanding of what you are good at before trying it; otherwise, don't bother because it's not worth the pain. I wouldn't try to be an actor because I can't act."

- Alexander McQueen –

About the Author

Nadja Solovieva graduated with a BA (Hons) degree in fashion from the renowned St. Martins College and trained at Alexander McQueen and Vivienne Westwood studios. She became an award-winning designer with her luxury accessories brand VASSILISA, featured in Elle and Vogue and retailing in some of the most prestigious stores on both sides of the Atlantic.

Being an international student, the author went through the whole process of foreign University application, English as a foreign language test, local education credits transfer, and portfolio making.

The advice she provides in this book for new talent finding their way into a fashion design career is second to none.

Table of Contents

Chapter 1

Design Calling

Talent and Natural Inclination to Create

There has always been a significant dispute on what constitutes talent, how much of it is reliant on practice, or whether it is simply an inborn ability. Another important notion in fashion is "good taste" which, considering stylistic differences in the modern world has become a relative notion. What remains a fact is that a fashion collection must appeal to a group of customers for it to be desirable enough to purchase and wear. A designer may build their own audiences to create for, or they may work for a fashion house that believes their style fits its audiences.

What one usually notices, about someone with an inherent talent to create fashion, is an inclination to be naturally expressive on their own, this often starts to show early on in life. An example being Michael Kors complete revamping of his mothers' wedding dress at the age of 5, a soul-touching fact in his biography.

Top fashion schools are highly skilled at spotting talent on entry. With as many as 100 applicants per place in some top fashion schools, admissions committee members are looking for a number of characteristics, including, but not limited to, the ability to generate original ideas, skills to communicate ideas visually, and the self-determination to produce creatively.

Disregarding style preference, every designer must have an eye for colour, shape and texture, to some degree of harmony, and must be able to communicate these ideas visually in order to make them into garments. Here, drawing skills are especially handy, as well as draping and others. These skills can be perfected through study and practice.

Not everything is lost if you come from a background where you were occluded from an opportunity to be creative. Some people come from suppressive environments. It is recommended to tap into creativity by:

- Doing short courses in schools you are thinking of applying to, online or in person.
- Drawing, photographing, keeping a creative diary or sketchbook, or doing practically anything creative.

Age is Not the Limit

A Fashion Undergraduate course usually consists, partly of students entering immediately after high school, and partly of students in their mid-late 20s who have worked or studied already, occasionally students in their 30s.

The Postgraduate MA fashion course usually consists of students entering directly after a BA degree, but more often, older students in their late 20s, 30s, and even 40s, who have worked in fashion and want to advance their proficiency, to re-qualify, or who are planning to create their own label.

Recently the actor Antonio Banderas followed his passion for menswear design by enrolling at St. Martins College, which made a bespoke program for him. Kanye West prior to launching his label came for an interview with the head of Fashion MA at St. Martins, who at the time was the legendary Louise Wilson. We do not know what happened between them, but Kanye launched his business without studying on the course.

An individual should not be restrained by age limits to pursue their talents. Giorgio Armani established his label only at the age of 41, creating one of the most successful fashion brands of our time. He had a medical degree and had served in the army (source: Business of Fashion).

Re-Qualifications

A significant number of fashion designers have originally studied something else. For example, Mary Katranzou, who currently designs for Bulgari, had a BA degree in architecture prior to changing to fashion design by doing a Fashion MA course at St. Martins. Tom Ford and Virgil Abloh were also trained as architects. Vera Wang, of the eponymous wedding dresses brand, spent years as a fashion editor at Vogue. In a rare occurrence, Pharrell Williams is a musician who is now a creative director at Louis Vuitton, owing to his exceptional modern taste. Multiple celebrities have turned their hand to fashion, including Kanye West and Kim Kardashian. These designers could probably be considered more fashion entre-preneurs or creative directors.

Segmentation in Fashion

Fashion design is a versatile skill, one can be working any-where from premium, to mid, and mass-market fashion seg-ments. A designer can relate to one audience more than an-other, and have more talent for a certain market segment. To grasp the difference between market segments, it is im-portant to understand the concept of "fashion trend cycles": the more premium fashion is, the more distinctive the identity is and the more skill is put into its original creative research and development. Other segments, mid and mass-fashion, are more interested in already existing trends and designing with those in mind, which is also a type of talent. In premium fashion, designers are more interested in the talent to create trends, rather than in following them. The founders of most heritage brands were unique visionaries, grasping something uniquely desirable for their generation and generations to come.

High Fashion

This is probably the market aspiring designers are most attracted to, due to the high degree of originality and possibility of self-expression. These are the fashion brands that entice millions of people with spectacular collections, shows and campaigns, venturing into a variety of products in the same brand spirit. Valentino, Versace, Lagerfeld, Chanel, Gucci etc. tempt us with new desirable fashion and accessories collections every season. High fashion brands have a unique story behind them and a highly distinctive brand DNA, which helps them to license this distinctive "brand spirit" into highly profitable products, such as perfume, cosmetics etc. They do not follow trends, but create them. Such brands' teams are exceptional, creatively and technically. Parisian and Italian brands most often own factories and production units, but outsourcing of production is also common. Designers working on the production side of fashion, for manufacturers, tend to be more technically inclined.

High Fashion is mostly associated with heritage brands such as Balenciaga, Dior, Chanel etc. which have long outlived their founders. These fashion houses employ outstanding designers and creative directors to keep the brand up-to-date in terms of relevance to the market, while preserving the original brand DNA, which the original founders had laid as a foundation. These are highly artistic designers who are able to play with a heritage brand's identity and interpret it in a modern manner which is desirable to consumers.

When one makes their name as a creative director for one of these heritage brands, one has reached the pinnacle of a fashion design career, the only step above would be to have one's own brand. Making a name as an employee for one of the "super brands" can lead to getting investors interested and launching one's own brand eventually. Career moves of top creative designers such as Raf Simmons, Alessandro Michele, Anthony Vaccarello, Matthieu Blazy etc. are big news and are closely watched by the industry.

Fashion houses usually spot talent from:

- Designers proving themselves and progressing on the corporate ladder in premium fashion from junior design and assistant positions. Most of them tend to have formal higher education.
- Designers who have their own label, and became known to press and industry with their own shows or campaigns, are sometimes invited to lead heritage fashion houses. From his own label Virgil Abloh went to Luis Vuitton, and Demna Gvasalia to Balenciaga.
- Winners and runners-up of prestigious fashion competitions, such as Hyeres or LVMH prize etc, whose collections caught the eye of fashion houses.
- Fashion graduates scouted directly from college, final shows and graduation exhibitions, where the industry is invited. This includes inquiries fashion labels place through college tutors, and course directors, with whom they studied themselves.
- Word of mouth is exceptionally important in the fashion industry.

Own Label in High Fashion

Creating one's own brand is often the ultimate dream for a designer. This can sound unattainable, but we have seen over only 20 years, that designers such as Tom Ford, Alexander McQueen and more, have worked to become leading luxury

brands with billion-dollar valuations. Some of these new luxury brands went on to be acquired by the biggest fashion and beauty conglomerates, including
LVMH, Kering, Richmond, Este Lauder and Capri Goup.

St. Martins College of Art and Design produced an unprecedented number of independent designers with their own labels, and not only stellar names such as John Galliano, Stella McCartney, Alexander McQueen, Christopher Kane etc. From my graduation year alone David Koma, Emilia Wickstead, Mark Fast, Francesca Liberatore, and VASSILISA, all became successful fashion labels which trade internationally. From the same year, Lotta Volkova went on to become a super stylist for super brands, such as Miu Miu.

Couture

High fashion houses used to make a lot of couture, but today few brands, such as Chanel, continue to keep small "made-to-order" departments for select important customers.

There exists a small number of designers who prefer to work as couturiers and run their own small ateliers, focusing on select customers and creating custom and fitted fashion for them.

Mid-Market Fashion

Mid-market fashion has changed in recent years. It is something in the 100-900 Dollars range. It can be an extension line of a high fashion brand, which does not use as expensive fabrics and technical solutions as the main line. It can be an interesting independent designer. It can be any label that has something more premium to offer, than the mass market, in terms of quality or unique identity.

While some mid-market fashion is flourishing (Michael Kors, Tory Burch, etc.), many independent mid-market labels went under in recent years. Mid-market fashion, at this price point, has to make something interesting and very good, which is often overly expensive to develop, unless financing and marketing budgets are fantastic - it is not always easy to manage.

Mass-Market Fashion

Mass-market fashion, Zara, H&M, Uniqlo, Mango, Primark etc., thrives on existing fashion trends, which come from earlier stages of the fashion cycle, from premium and mid fashion designers. Mass-market fashion companies have powerful and optimised production, logistics and distribution, which allow for large volumes of production and low prices. It does not invest in original creative research and development, as high fashion does. Mass-market companies scout and employ talented designers, but they mostly work to spot existing trends, often from the fashion shows of others, and re-interpret them. Mass-market brands do not have their own highly distinctive brand DNA, they select what is currently in trend and cater to consumer demand. It is big business.

Onacio Ortega, who owns Zara as part of his Inditex group with other brands, is as wealthy as Bill Gates. He started making clothes in the 1970s and does not have professional designer qualifications.

Counterfeit, Overstock, etc.

Lowest of the chain, where no creative talent wants to be.

Types of Fashion Designer

When one wants to be a fashion designer, one may not necessarily think how many interesting and exciting variations of fashion design exist. One may need to explore this in advance, because most fashion colleges only accept BA degree applications for an already known speciality. At St. Martins, for example, one is applying specifically for a Fashion Degree in Design in:

- Womenswear
- Menswear
- Knitwear
- Fashion Print
- Textiles Design (a separate division from Fashion School)

Besides the most popular womenswear design, there are a number of fascinating fashion design specialties to get into eventually:

- Lingerie
- Sportswear
- Soft Accessories (scarves etc.)
- Accessories, Leather goods (bags, wallets, belts, etc.)
- Footwear
- Children's wear etc.

One may get passionate about one of these design specialties, as a compass for future employment or one's own business.

Design Graduate Case Study: "Originally, I was most interested in Knitwear design, with my mom taking me to Sonia Rykiel's boutique in the '90s. I thought that luxurious, elegant and comfortable jersey, as was the quality at the time, was the way to dress. Printed fashion was not particularly my interest; however, this is what emerged as a prominent note in my graduation collection, and print became the core of my fashion accessories label."

Fashion Design Positions

Fashion Creative Director

Similar to the post of a head designer, but even broader artistically speaking, where one has to oversee various collections of a brand, as well as the whole brand identity and its consistency across all products, lines, and campaigns. In this role there is so much to manage that there are multiple designers working underneath on ideas and designs, which the creative director now "filters", amends, and brings up to standard, and others execute the vision. A creative director continuously participates in the line-ups of main collections, extension lines, accessories, etc. In fashion, this senior role would usually be filled by someone who has a background in fashion design, but not always.

In France and Italy, one can hear a designer being addressed as a styliste, e.g. Karl Lagerfeld, meaning "styliste de mode" – "a designer" in French. This is different in the UK and USA, where a designer is someone who creates clothes, while a stylist is someone who arranges existing clothes and dresses clients for photoshoots, appearances, and simply for life.

One usually becomes a creative director after decades of experience and with an exceptional set of abilities and connections. Karl Lagerfeld was a creative director extraordinaire. It may sound unattainable to helm a super brand, but Matthieu Blazy has just become the creative director of Chanel at only 32 years of age.

Fashion Designer

A fashion designer creates clothes or accessories in the context of a seasonal collection and the whole brand vision. Fashion design can be more artistic or technical. It includes research, development, concepts, fabrics and trimmings selection etc. A designer communicates designs, usually through illustrations and technical drawings.

Junior Designer

Most advertised junior designer positions in mass or mid-market brands, these days, also require at least a Fashion Bachelor's Degree.

Different Facets of a Designer

The profession of Fashion Designer deals with creation of a product, which involves various people for the final result to be reached. A designer is an artist, a team member, and a bundle of many talents.

Fashion Designer as an Artist

Sometimes, when someone hears that you are a fashion designer, they ask: "so how many designs have you sketched today?" This couldn't be further from the reality of complex design processes, which entail in-depth authentic visual research, extraction of the most relevant lines of inspiration for the next and future seasons, concept formation and colour palettes – this happens before one even lifts a pen or a pencil to sketch anything.

This outlines the importance of a team to support the designer, particularly during their immersion into the design process, to continue managing all business aspects, advertising and selling.

Designer as an Entrepreneur

Although this book mostly addresses "becoming a designer" in terms of becoming a creative who is trained to envision and design collections, it is also important to remember that fashion is a business, which is a creative endeavour in its own right. For some designers who launch and grow their own business, the administration and business side of things begins to outweigh most of the time and effort, so that it starts making more sense to employ designers who meticulously focus only on design. It is here, in the fast-moving and high-pressure environment of a growing business, that prior training as a designer comes in handy, as one can swiftly oversee, correct and choose skilfully, thanks to one's training in design.

Even if a designer does not run their own fashion company, they would benefit from some degree of business skills to progress their own career, position themself, and create desirability for their own products and skills.

One can do some self-education on business and fashion entrepreneurship skills through short practical courses on platforms, such as Foundr, which spot some of the most recent trends and immediate opportunities in online marketing and social media, or through in-depth academic entrepreneurship studies. Professor Neri Karra explores the entrepreneurship phenomena in her books, such as "Fashion Entrepreneurship" and "Pioneers", where she also looks into related aspects such as immigration and cultural diversity.

Some University degrees devoted to business, come with a fashion or luxury angle. Some examples:

Regents University (UK) BA "Business and Luxury Brand Management".
Marangoni University (Italy) Master's Degree "Fashion Start-Up".
Bocconi (Italy) Master in Fashion, Experience & Design Management.
INSEAD (France) Master in Management.
Stern Business School (USA) MBA "Business: Luxury & Retail."

Fashion Designer as Social Personality

Some designers are very sociable, and it becomes a part of their brand's DNA and unique story. Such as the legendary Diane Von Furstenberg. Some designers can be more reclusive, but anyone who has their own business has to be socially active, or have someone active on their behalf, to build and maintain cooperative relationships bridging their creations with the world.

Other Factors in a Design Career

Other factors in a designer's career can play a significant role, particularly if one decides to make it on their own with their own label.

Family and Eco system

Be it emotionally or financially a designer's most important supporters are usually their family or partner. This support is often key in the decision to pursue, or not to pursue the challenge of starting one's own fashion business. Family is the most usual source of early financial assistance.

In Italy, fashion is often a family business continued from generation to generation. And fashion and textiles have been major industries for hundreds of years. One only needs to watch the recent Gucci film, to get an idea about Italian fashion dynasties. This tradition kept running with the example of the Versace family. While Gianni was the genius designer, his brother Santo built the business, which was later creatively directed by their sister Donatella until the brand's later acquisition by Kering. Miuccia Prada studied political science and theatre, but soon joined her family's business which specialised in manufacturing luxury leather bags, to bring it to the new levels of success, which Prada and Miu Miu enjoy now. Patrizio Bertelli, Miucia's husband, is responsible for the commercial side of products as well as company strategy, as per the Prada website.

Internationally, multiple brands are founded and run by siblings or husband-and-wife duos. American brand Rodarte is designed by sisters Kate and Laura Mulleavy. DSquared is helmed by twin brothers Dean and Dan Caten. The beautiful Zimmerman brand is successfully created and run by two Australian sisters, Nicky and Simone, for the last three decades.

When becoming a fashion designer, it is a good idea to consider family and personal environment factors, to help create a support system that allows talent to flourish.

Home Country Opportunities

Although all high fashion seems to be happening in Paris, Milan, London, and NYC, with leading fashion weeks taking place there, some of the best fashion business opportunities can be found in lesser known, developing regions.

One has to remember that after graduating, even from the most prestigious college, if the job opportunity does not come along immediately, it can be very expensive to continue to stay in that city/country, and there may be some other hard limiting factors in getting a job or starting a business, such as visas etc. It is recommended to research and get an idea of opportunities in one's own country, and scout businesses that may be interested in your skills after obtaining a fashion degree.

Some of the most fascinating fashion business opportunities occur in the lesser known and emerging markets, which are not as saturated as established economies. Here one can identify high-potential, niches of customers.

Networking and Personality

Designers are often introverted or shy personalities, which is not unusual for creative people. These designers tend to have business partners or PRs who can handle communications on their behalf. Based on personality traits, some designers may be more comfortable being employed by others, which helps to avoid multiple social interactions associated with managing and promoting a business.

Student Social Case Study: "While I was a student at St. Martins, I was lucky to be accidentally seated close to John Galliano in a central London Cafe. While it was probably too much for me to ask for an internship, it still made a deep impression on me to receive some words of encouragement from him".

Test It

If one is seriously considering a future in fashion and to proceed with the 3-4 year commitment as well as the expenses of a Bachelor's Degree, it is a good idea for a future fashion designer to at least get a glimpse of this business by interning or working in it for a short period, such as a few weeks, or even a few days.

Practical Experience

While still in high school, and with parental consent, one can do a short internship with a local fashion designer or boutique. A first step would be to call or visit a selected designer studio or shop. If the owner is not there, one can leave a note, reminiscent of a future "Cover Letter", with information about yourself, why you admire this particular designer or store, how many weeks you are prepared to work or intern there, and your contact details. One can be lucky to find the fashion designer or the shop owner there on the shop floor, or at their office. Some designers and shop owners can be very friendly, and some are less so, this will depend on factors like everyday stress associated with their business. In my experience, designers enjoy encouraging and supporting talented young individuals who are passionate about the business, have a friendly personality and are willing to learn.

A stint as a sales assistant in a local boutique provides insight into the fashion and retail business. You never know who can walk in through that door and who can become your future customer or supporter. Some of the most prestigious stores, such as Harrods and Harvey Nichols, are taking extra part-time staff for busy times of the year, particularly Christmas and Easter.

Work experience in fashion, is not an exception to the principle that one is likely to learn more and gain deeper insight into company operations, by being in a smaller company as opposed to a big corporation.

Summer School and Short Courses

Attending summer fashion school, which can last 4 to 10 weeks, is also an option if you want to get an idea of what awaits in a fashion job. By doing courses, one can understand better the different angles of fashion, and whether the "crafty" bit - the fashion design itself - is truly what one wants to pursue. Otherwise, one may discover talents which fit other niches within the fashion industry, such as marketing, entrepreneurship or management.

Fashion Libraries and Open Sources

It is a good idea to experience fashion school atmosphere, by visiting its libraries and reading and studying there. All University of Arts Libraries, which include London College of Fashion and Central Saint Martin's libraries, are open to all visitors to use their collections for research, with a booking, as per the UAL website.

It is interesting to study and read the history of heritage brands and designers that inspire you. Biographies of designers such as Coco Chanel, Christian Dior and Yves Saint Laurent are the subject of multiple books and films (some mentioned in the Reference section of this book).

Chapter 2

Related Fashion Careers

Sometimes one knows they want to be in fashion, however the area where your talent lies may not be in fashion design itself. There are a variety of related creative careers: stylist, fashion editor, buyer, visual merchandiser, to name a few.

In recent years, we have seen a number of celebrities and social media influencers becoming fashion designers.

Celebrity

Only a couple of decades ago, actors and singers only used to endorse designers. Now, with increased social media dialogue with audiences, it's become a logical step for many celebrities, who already have their own audience base, to launch their own fashion labels.

Victoria Beckham, who originally rose to fame as a singer, became passionately focused on her namesake label and being a fashion designer. As well as Kanye West with Yeezy, Kim Kardashian with Skims, and many other multitalented people. The advantage these individuals have is that they are already well acquainted with publicity mechanisms, have teams and contacts, as well as streams of income to finance their fashion endeavour.

There isn't yet a label, designed by a celebrity, which has been acquired by a major luxury fashion group such as Kering or LVMH, to join the ranks of premium designer fashion. Newly acquired brands still tend to be solemnly focused on fashion designers. That being said, in the fast-changing fashion world everything is possible.

Social Media Influencer

We have seen the same trend occurring with social media influencers and bloggers, who have their own substantial base of followers. Not necessarily all audiences are potential fashion consumers. Chiara Ferragni and Aimee Song, are among successful bloggers, who have launched their own labels. Influencers often get into this business because of their passion for design, or simply because a fashion manufacturer who is looking for audiences approaches them and offers them a good deal. An influencer might not necessarily have enough time to devote to design, so in this case there would be designers on the side of a manufacturer, who are able to reflect on a blogger's style.

Classic Fashion Professions

Fashion Stylist

A fashion stylist is someone who works with existing clothes to create visual communication: as applied to magazine pictures, promotion campaigns and celebrity appearances. It is a sought-after talent. Stylists can be employed to advise on fashion collections, most usually at the collection editing stage, when it heads towards photoshoots and campaign creation. Super stylists like Joe McKenna and Katie Grand are highly respected in the industry and command substantial fees. This career sometimes leads to the creation of one's own fashion magazine.

There are fashion styling courses in fashion colleges, such as Vogue College, but many super stylists started simply from their motivation to do photoshoots and work with photographers. Many stylists have Art or Fashion Design degrees, such as British super stylist Katie Grand whose degree is in fashion print.

Creative Pattern Cutter

A pattern cutter makes shapes of clothes on card or paper from a design sketch or a drape on a mannequin. Some prominent designers come from more of a pattern-cutting and draping background, than sketching. Their collections tend to be "pattern-led", focused on exquisite shapes and fit, such as Rick Owen and Todd Lynn. Every Fashion Design BA course includes a pattern cutting stint, but it takes years of experience to achieve real proficiency in pattern-cutting, as it is a talent of its own. Good pattern cutting is worth its weight in gold.

These days, most advertised positions for a pattern cutting job also require formal education, i.e. at least a 2 years HND (High National Diploma in the UK). Central St. Martins College has a Creative Pattern Cutting Diploma course.

Buyer

A buyer works for a store or a retail group, they are the ones who decide on matters such as choice of brands, they estimate and plan quantities, and order collections seasonally. A buyer must have good taste appealing to their market. They must also have a swift eye and sensitivity to the demands of the market. Few know how mathematical and figures-driven the job of a buyer really is, involving endless spreadsheets of stock analysis and projections. Some buyer positions, particularly in department stores, require a mathematics test for the job.

The London College of Fashion (UK) and Fashion Institute of Technology (USA), offer industry renowned courses on fashion buying and merchandising. One can apply for a fashion buyer job directly on many employers' websites, such as major department stores.

Visual Merchandiser

A visual merchandiser is someone who creatively presents collections in store and its windows displays. The artistry of visual merchandising in stores creates a big buzz, notably Harvey Nichols seasonal window displays which are famous for their beauty and creativity. It's not unusual to spot Giorgio Armani contemplating displays in the windows of his Milan store.

Personal Stylist

A personal stylist helps to style individual for a particular occasion or simply in day-to-day life. The stylist selects and combines clothes from suitable brands, into looks which suit the body shape of a client and satisfy their objectives to look or feel a certain way. This can be very lucrative. L'Wren Scott was an American fashion designer who came from a successful styling, as well as modelling, background.

Fashion Editor

A fashion editor works with fashion, choosing which brands and looks to feature in a magazine or any fashion publication. Editors have a discerning eye for trends, clothing fit and colours. Fashion editors usually come from either journalistic or styling backgrounds. Some fashion designers, but not as many as one may expect, were editors, such as Vera Wang and Tabitha Simmons.

The brainchild of Conde Nast (the publisher of Vogue, Vanity Fair, GQ) - Vogue College of Fashion - offers courses teaching how to become a fashion editor or a stylist. Along with other fashion colleges such as Marangoni.

Fashion Illustrator

Some designers excel at fashion sketching, but while it is unusual to hear of a fashion illustrator becoming a fashion designer, there is a reverse trend of fashion designers going into art and illustration.

It is recommended for a future fashion designer to practice drawing and research illustration styles from beautiful sources such as FIDA Worldwide.

Sales Assistant

The path of fashion designer or fashion entrepreneur has never been straightforward. Michael Kors dropped out from the Fashion Institute of Technology in NYC in the 80s, and went to work in sales and merchandising in a boutique, where he met a lady who introduced his designs to Bergdorf & Goodman leading to him selling his line there (Source: Harper's Bazaar).

Donna Karen, in her autobiography "My Journey", highly praises her experience working as a sales assistant on a shop floor in NYC and highly recommends it to any future fashion designer wishing to understand the reality of the business, through interaction with real customers.

Store Owner

A store owner often acts in many roles simultaneously: as a creative director overseeing the whole concept, as a buyer, a visual merchandiser, a sales assistant, and even a personal stylist, from time to time. It may sound logical for a store owner to become a fashion designer, with their own fashion label to stock in store, but in reality, both professions are so overwhelming and time-consuming, that this happens very rarely.

Related Business Careers

Fashion business disciplines, such as business management, are often taught in the same colleges as fashion design. Schools such as Parsons, Fashion Institute of Technology, Marangoni, London College of Fashion. However, many senior fashion executives and businessmen in retail and fashion graduated from "non-fashion" universities, such as Stern Business School in the States, or the Ecole Polytechnique in France to name a few.

Fashion PR

Public Relations is a fascinating career path. In luxury fashion, PR is usually narrowly specialised to this segment, it being an exclusive world built of long-standing relationships. One can apply for an internship with a fashion PR agency to get an idea.

Fashion Retail Management

Various fashion or business schools offer a major in fashion retail management. Many senior retail managers, and even CEOs, progressed to this position having started out working on the shop floor.

Fashion CEO - Chief Executive Officer

Fashion CEOs often have a university undergraduate degree or a postgraduate degree, sometimes more than one. Some legendary CEOs came up through the ranks of retail management to arrive at this level. One can study the career path and education of their favourite fashion brands' CEOs, as this information is available on the internet and LinkedIn profiles.

Fashion CMO – Chief Marketing Officer

A CMO will often have a university degree, or even a postgraduate degree such as an MBA (Master of Business Administration), and have extensive experience in the industry.

Fashion Investor or Venture Capitalist

Many fashion businessmen graduated from universities, business schools, and MBA programs.

Chapter 3

Skills and How to Obtain Them

Besides an eye for proportion, colour, and texture - a designer must be able to express their ideas and designs in a comprehensive way, so as for others to understand and produce the physical objects envisioned. The designer communicates through practices such as drawing, collages, concept boards, draping and pattern cutting.

Drawing

A fashion designer is not an illustrator, and their drawings do not have to be a work of art, however often they look as such. The purpose of a fashion sketch is primarily, to communicate what is going on in the design: the overall silhouette, how the garment is approximately constructed, proportions and volumes, where seams are, position of the pockets, etc. A portfolio of a fashion school applicant is expected to already show high proficiency in drawing and other visual communication. A fashion collection should be presented drawn on a figure, with additional technical drawings, which explain each garment construction in further detail.

Fashion drawings tend to be "stylised" - one can study various, including the most up-to-date fashion illustration trends on platforms such as FIDA, which is dedicated to featuring the best talent.

It can be extremely useful to lay the foundations of drawing skills by attending drawing classes from figure, with anatomy study included if possible. Fashion, or even academic drawing, is rarely a part of a high school curriculum, but life drawing is often available in independent local drawing studios. In London, the Royal Academy of Arts offers affordable drop-in drawing sessions, as well as the Mall Galleries and local community centres.

It is important not to get into despair over drawing skills. There is also a concept of using "fashion dollies" — which are figure templates to draw on — not unusual in fashion. Some fashion designers are not avid drawers and are still able to produce fashion collections.

Practicing designer case study: "As a teenager I attended evening classes in a local drawing studio for years, because I felt it was helping me to express myself creatively and feel better. It turned out extremely useful when I went to study at fashion school and became a professional designer."

Research & Concept Skills

The originality and uniqueness of concepts are what distinguishes high fashion from mid and mass-market fashion. The uniqueness of a brand, so-called brand DNA, is felt through its collections, shows, campaigns, and everything that a brand does. Brand DNA is the essence making a brand memorable, distinct, and loved by current and potential audiences.

Successful fashion designers have a method of research, concept and design. Often with their favourite sources of inspiration and research. One could occasionally run into John Galliano in his former college library when he was already a world-renowned designer.

The so-called "sketchbook method" of creative research and design, which is taught in St. Martins College of Art and Design, is used by most of its graduates, many of whom are leading designers and fashion directors in the industry. This method teaches only to use original and historical sources of inspiration, not the already existing collections of other fashion designers, nor fashion magazines and other sources. A designer translates these original lines of inspiration into ideas of shape, colour and texture — identifying the best and most desirable ideas and combinations. Based on these lines a fashion collection is created.

For an aspiring fashion designer, it is recommended to collect visual inspiration from many sources, and start to translate these "impressions" into ideas, concepts, and actual fashion. It is recommended to attend exhibitions, theatre, inspiring places, and to read.

It is usual for fashion designers and high fashion houses to visit flea markets, such as Portobello Road Market, and visit second-hand shops for research, when starting to work on a new collection.

There are short courses which teach concept development, how to do creative research, and how to work with a sketchbook. These skills are taught in-depth during a BA degree course, culminating in a fashion collection.

Draping on a Stand

Fashion is a 3D creation. Shapes and silhouettes are crucial in fashion design. The renowned Dior 1950s silhouette, set the trend for the whole era. Chanel became distinct as a brand through revolutionising the silhouettes of her era, which remain to this day an essential part of the brand's DNA.

For many designers, draping on a mannequin, sometimes in exaggerated form, is essential for their design development processes. These forms are able to create an impressive visual impact in catwalk shows, such as the exaggerated shoulders in recent Balenciaga shows etc. Draping is a part of any fashion design degree. Some designers' methods are very much based on draping, while others find sketching more native for their design process and expression.

It can be handy to buy a tailor's mannequin or to borrow one, to drape on and take pictures to use in a fashion portfolio.

Pattern Cutting

Clothes are 3D in shape, but the shape is created from flat 2D. Pattern cutting is becoming computerised, like everything else in the modern world. However high-end fashion still tends to create patterns on paper and card, as this is a big part of a design process and experiment. Pattern cutting is an essential part of any fashion design degree course.

Not every designer can do pattern cutting themselves to perfection. There are skilled pattern cutters who have done only that for decades. It must be stressed that good pattern cutting is worth its weight in gold.

CAD

CAD (Computer Aided Design programs) tends to be more actively used for mass-produced goods, accessories and sportswear for example. Adobe Illustrator, Photoshop, and Procreate are very useful for creative processes, drawing, and collaging, as well as specialist programs for fashion design technical drawings and pattern-cutting. With AI technologies continue evolving.

Business and Management Skills

To some degree, any fashion designer, particularly the one planning to take a more entrepreneurial route, needs business skills, even if it is just for salary negotiation in one's own employment. Fashion is a fast-paced business that engages teams of people though various stages of a products creation and delivery and it is essential to develop the abilities to work in a team, be resilient to stress and be good at multitasking.

Languages

One should be able to speak the language of the country where their fashion college or future employer will be located. If one is interested in working for a luxury heritage brand, most are still based in France or Italy. English is spoken across borders, and it is essential to be proficient.

Routes of Skills Attainment

Apprenticeship

Before fashion began to be produced industrially in volume, fashion designers were traditionally tailors, and the fashion design profession was not a discipline of higher education. Knowledge and skills were mostly obtained and passed down through apprenticeship, and by learning practically how clothes were made and a business was run.

Ungaro was an apprentice to Balenciaga, Yves Saint Laurent started with mundane tasks for Christian Dior, and Gianni Versace was an apprentice in a seamstress workshop belonging to his mother. These days, however, it is hard even to secure an unpaid internship, unless one is a fashion degree student. Fashion schools are often well-connected and can arrange internships in fashion houses for their students.

Owning a Business

One inevitably trains in design skills when one runs their own fashion label, where there is more control how to design and how to communicate creative ideas into existence. The originality of these processes can sometimes exceed expectations.

Coco Chanel was, as the legend says, raised by the nuns who taught her how to sew, and she never sought any other fashion education or training with anyone. She continues to be considered one of the most successful designers of all time.

Short Courses

Short courses are fantastic for helping get an idea of one or several specific subjects in fashion, or to perfect a specific skill. Recently, a lawyer friend asked me if one can become a fashion designer by doing short courses only. Historically, one could become a fashion designer without any course at all, though apprenticeship. Looking at fashion positions advertised today, they all predominantly require a fashion BA degree as an absolute necessity. Knowing how strenuous and competitive fashion studies are, short courses are usually not enough, unless one is more of a fashion design entrepreneur, and already employs the correct teams.

Formal Higher Education

Those who become prominent fashion designers tend to have a university degree in some subject. There are a number of famous designers with unfinished degrees, because something in their career took off prior to completion of studies, or they simply decided formal education was not for them.

A recently successful French designer Simon Porte Jacquemus studied at fashion school for only 3 months, declaring himself to be "underwhelmed by academic studies", according to L'Officiel magazine.

The main types of higher education courses which prepare students for a career in fashion design are:

High National Diploma (HND) Course duration is 2 academic years. Graduates can go straight into employment, finding jobs such as design room assistants, garment technologists, stylists, fashion allocators, merchandisers, buyers, or retail managers.

Bachelor's Degree (BA) Completed in 3-4 years full-time and usually required for most advertised fashion design positions.

Master of Arts Degree (MA) A post-graduate degree in Fashion, which takes 1-2 academic Years. It is 17 months full-time in St. Martins.

Based on various case studies, a formal education in fashion is not obligatory for success. Many well-to-do fashion designers and entrepreneurs succeeded without it, or with a degree in a different discipline. However, if one analyses the current fashion jobs market and the positions advertised, it is hard to find any position that does not require at least a

Bachelor degree (BA). For this reason, it is the degree we are mostly focusing on in this book and in the next chapter.

Chapter 4

Formal Education

How to Choose a Fashion School

A fashion school is only as good as its graduates. One can find various rankings for fashion schools on the internet, but one must remember that rankings can also be a product of PR. The best idea is to take your favourite designers and see in which fashion schools they studied. Although it may have been a while ago and things may have changed. Some courses can be renowned, only because of a specific fashion tutor or course director. That said, leading colleges are doing their best to maintain their reputation by consistently maintaining a high teaching level.

An important aspect here is that graduates of a particular fashion school like to employ other graduates from the same school, possibly because of familiarity with the same "shared" methods of research and design. Graduates who work in fashion houses or have their own labels often stay in contact with their college tutors, or course directors, and keep an ear to the ground for prospective talent in this way.

Top fashion schools include, but are not limited to:

- Central St. Martins College of Art & Design in London (part of UAL University of Arts London) has produced a phenomenal number of industry names, particularly those who went on to launch their own successful brands such as Alexander Mc Queen, John Galliano, Stella McCartney, Christopher Kane, to name a few.
- Parsons School of Design, whose graduates include Marc Jacobs, Alexander Wang and Anna Sui.
- Fashion Institute of Technology NYC, alma mater of Calvin Klein, Michael Kors and Norma Kamali.
- Antwerp Fashion Academy (Part of the Royal Academy of Fine Arts, in Belgium). Graduates include Dries Van Noten, Martin Mariela and Demna Gvasalia.

The fees of highly ranked schools' may be very similar to those of not-so-highly ranked, so why not try to get into the fashion school of your dreams. That being said, some very successful designers, such as Kate Spade and Tory Burch, went to lesser-known schools in fashion.

Home or Abroad

Some of the best schools can be located in a different town, country or continent from yourself and unfortunately, living and travel expenses can add up. On the other hand, 3 beautiful years living in a multicultural city such as London, Paris, Milan or NYC can be the experience of a lifetime, meeting people and making friends for life from all over the world. On the other hand, for some students living abroad can be a hard and lonely experience. Good schools usually have student services which can help.

Some fashion schools, like Instituto Marangoni, offer courses in different locations around the world: Milan, Florence, Paris, London, Miami, Mumbai, Shanghai, and Shenzhen. This number of locations simplifies the application process, and makes studying fashion more local and accessible.

One can study fashion design close to home, as well as doing a period of study abroad in a fashion capital. It is a new practice offered by several colleges. Central St. Martins College offers an Advanced Fashion Design Semester: a 13-week course created to give students from abroad an authentic Saint Martin's fashion design experience, using experimental research and design development techniques that are original and innovative. All courses are assessed, and students receive a record of study at the end of the programme to request credit from their home institution. Other colleges also offer similar programs and modules.

Prior to Committing

Contact your chosen fashion schools about their requirements to estimate if you have enough time to prepare everything necessary before the application deadline. Ideally, visit the school and its neighbourhood, prior to committing to 3 years, particularly if it is a long-distance relocation.

Find out how your fashion school is organised into faculties and divisions and what fashion specialisations are offered, in order to tailor your portfolio and cover letter for your chosen option. A portfolio for a Knitwear Design division would be very different to a portfolio for Menswear Design, or Fashion Print for example.

Preparatory Courses

There are various short courses that can help specifically towards application and building a fashion portfolio. Most often these are: drawing for fashion, concept, basics of design etc. Many of these courses are available online.

It is crucial to create a strong fashion portfolio for university application. Unfortunately, fashion is a subject that is usually not taught in high school, and one must pursue their passion independently. The graduation exhibitions of many colleges provide examples of student portfolios. These exhibitions usually take place in June and one can sign up to attend. Examples of portfolios can also sometimes be available at colleges' Open Days, specifically hosted for new applicants and these usually take place in Spring.

There are courses specifically tailored towards creating a Fashion Portfolio, such as a one-year Fashion Folio Course at St. Martins, which "will result in a portfolio for application to degree courses, employment or self-development". One can contact local, or not-so-local fashion schools, about short courses aimed at helping specifically with portfolio building. It can be extremely helpful and motivating to work on a portfolio in a group, if the course is not online.

Finances

Studying fashion at university is a significant investment. A fashion BA course usually takes 3 years. 4 years if it is a special program, such as a "sandwich course" including 1-year of work experience in the industry. The cost of an academic year can vary anywhere from 12-50 thousand dollars, depending on the school and the country it is in. One should contact schools to find out their exact and current fees, as they are subject to change. Course fees will not include materials, accommodation and other living expenses.

Loans are the usual way of financing any University degree. Specifically, the UK government's Student Finance England offers tuition fee loans as well as potentially offering maintenance loans to help cover both tuition and living costs. International students may have access to private lending, if they have a UK guarantor. In the USA there are federal and private loan options.

Scholarships & Grants are not as widely available for fashion as they are for some other disciplines, such as Science. Grants are more likely to be available for domestic and state students, rather than international applicants, but there are still opportunities for extremely talented international students. For example, Instituto Marangoni offers scholarships through talent contests. In America, information is available on the websites of organisations such as the Council of Fashion Designers of America and the Fashion Scholarship Fund. Programs and scholarships change from year to year. One should contact all the Universities one is interested in, as well as all the external foundations one can find, to inquire about grant opportunities.

Some websites to search for Scholarships are: Bachelor Portal, Masters Portal, and We Make Scholars.

Higher education is a significant investment to make.

Entry Requirements

There can be as many as 120 initial applications per place in a prestigious fashion school for a BA or MA degree. It is not difficult to enter if you have talent, perseverance, and a strong work ethic. Admission committees will see by the quality of work, the amount of hours you have put into the creation of a fashion portfolio.

One has to check with each school specifically, as it can vary slightly from school to school and country to country. Application requirements typically include:

Fashion Portfolio: Has to be strong and demonstrate not only talent, but discipline and the ability to follow guidelines.

Sufficient academic standard: An official record of good grades from one's previous education, typically high school, or previous University. If academic records are from overseas, grades would need to be translated. If providing copies, or translating from a different grading system, they may need to be notarized.

Statement of Purpose: An essay elaborating why you are applying to this particular school, and motivations for wanting to be a fashion designer. Elaborating on your passion and commitment to be a good fashion student and future fashion designer.

Recommendations: Ideally from 2-3 people who know you stating why you would be a good student for this school, and a great fashion designer, eventually.

English as a foreign language test: sufficient score. When applying to an education institution in an English-speaking country, the test is usually IELTS (International English Language Testing System). It can be taken domestically at allocated centres in your country. Depending on current language proficiency, one may need to take a language course or private tuition, to prepare for the test. Language proficiency requirements are increasingly required by some UK fashion colleges.

Unconditional or Conditional Offer

Upon acceptance you will receive either one of these offers from a Fashion School. An unconditional offer means you are good to go as soon as you submit payment. A conditional offer means acceptance depends on presentation of some additional criteria which are not yet fulfilled and you will have time to send it in. For example, obtaining a satisfactory IELTS language score result.

Visas

Upon receiving Place Confirmation from a College, an international student can apply for a Student Visa in an embassy of their home country. This process comes with additional requirements, such as showing proof of funds for the whole length of study, which can be bank statements or an official letter from a parent or sponsor. Sometimes, a student Visa allows one to work a certain number of hours per week. Considering a BA course is full-time and expensive, one needs to determine how time is best allocated.

Portfolio

A fashion college applicant is presenting a portfolio, which is usually required to include:

- 3-4 distinctive fashion collections.
- 10-15 fashion looks per collection.
- A3 or A4 size is usually a standard.

- Each collection comes with a page demonstrating the concept.
- Portfolio pages presenting designs, on a figure, with swatches of fabric and trimmings, as well as technical drawings explaining construction.

A lesser-known tip: tutors love to see alternate expressions of creativity as part of the application, alongside a formal portfolio. If you photograph - include photography. If you paint - include pictures of your paintings. If you do embroidery, knit, or sculpture – make sure to include pictures or examples of them.

Portfolios are always shipped by recorded post, with specific labelling, as advised by a fashion school.

Application

Process. While in most countries, BA degree applications are done directly to the University, these days, it is conveniently done through an online form. In the UK all BA applications are made through UCAS (the Universities and Colleges Admissions Service). This is the organisation that manages applications for undergraduate courses at universities and colleges in the UK. It essentially serves as a central platform for students to apply to multiple institutions with a single application. Students may select up to 5 courses in different schools.

Timing. Applications for an academic year beginning in September, should be received by Spring. A reasonable time to start preparation is by the spring of the previous year, if not sooner. Consider that you will be juggling your current school final exams with creating a fashion portfolio, and preparing for an English language test, if you are foreign, all at the same time. It is a lot to handle.

Helpful Resources for Overseas Students

If possible, it is highly recommended to visit the school you are applying to in advance. Universities host Open Days, usually held in springtime, where you can see examples of portfolios and speak with alumni, professors, and course directors.

International students can get help in British or American Education Centres, available in many countries, which have libraries with details about universities, fees, and grants. They usually provide information about the English as a foreign language test, or even hold those tests there.

International Student Case Study: "When I applied to UAL at the end of the 90s, it was quite a story. As it was pre-internet times, an application had to be sent via an international recorded delivery. As a teenager, I walked for 20 minutes in the snow along some scary highway to reach the only UPS office in the city at the time. Although I studied English at school, I had difficulty understanding many words and terminology. No one had heard about collecting and translating education credits into English. Places that helped were the British Education Council and the American Education Centre, both of which had libraries with university catalogues. I passed my IELTS English language exam there too".

What's in a BA Fashion Course

A BA degree is usually 3 academic years, 4 years if it is a course with a unique programme, such as a sandwich course with a 1-year internship in the industry.

Students are taught:
- Hands-on fundamentals of dressmaking: construction, draping, pattern cutting, and sewing.
- Artistic aspects of research and design.
- Art and Fashion History and Theory.

Creative experimentation with shape and texture culminates with the renowned "White Fashion Show" at the end of the first year at St. Martins, where students present a capsule collection in white "toile" fabric, demonstrating first steps in developing their own style, in terms of silhouette and texture. Colours are not involved at this stage.

BA course students are taught artistic aspects of design:

- Creative research from original sources, presented in the form of highly artistic sketchbooks.
- Original concept development.
- Designing and sampling a highly artistic collection.
- Presenting and documenting a collection, creatively and coherently with a concept.

Some design projects in the Undergraduate degree include studying the work of a specific fashion house, most often heritage, and designing a collection for it, to train students to grasp another brand's DNA and how to design for others. Other projects require a design student to focus on their own original distinctive style.

You will be taught some history of fashion and its evolution, and essays will be written.

At the end of a course, a fashion design graduate should be able to produce:

- A fashion collection of approximately 20 total fashion looks.
- Fashion accessories, if a designer wants them for the concept.
- A fashion show, which a college usually organises with select graduate collections.
- A presentation at the Graduates Exhibition.
- Collection campaign visuals: usually photography using life models, stylistically aligned with the concept.
- A portfolio and sketchbooks, which demonstrate creative thinking and design process. Fashion houses are interested in these development materials.

This graduation collection is very important because it lays the foundation of a designer's individual style. These visuals become the first portfolio to be shown to potential employers.

Original Research

Without going into the details of high-fashion design methods taught in top fashion schools, it can be said that a good fashion collection would have at least 4 original lines of inspiration, which are selected from an even wider scope of creative research. For design-led fashion, sources of research cannot be fashion magazines or collections of other brands. Original sources of inspiration should be evident.

Albert Elbaz, a legendary creative director for Lanvin, said in his talk at the London College of Fashion that it was not a secret that some of the leading fashion houses in the world start their collections design from research trips to Portobello market in London.

While in College

Numerous designers met their fashion business partners in college. American duo, Jack McCollough and Lazaro Hernandez met while studying together at Parsons School of Design and collaborating on their thesis, which became their first collection as Proenza Schouler brand. Alexander McQueen studied with fellow St. Martins student Sarah Burton, who later became head designer of his brand.

It is strongly recommended to network across your college faculty divisions, such as photography, journalism, promotion and go to student parties. At this time these are the best resources one can have. Photography, styling and makeup students also need material for their portfolios. Keep an eye out for those who could be your potential models.

Accommodation During Studies

Fashion schools, like most universities, have a housing office department, which can be very helpful.

Flat sharing can make life more fun. Your flatmates are likely to continue careers in the same industry, and to become well-known designers, popular stylists, journalists. Even if one goes back to one's own country after studying, one will have made dear friendships for life. This makes study in a cosmopolitan city, such as London, the experience of a lifetime.

Employment During a Degree

Student Visas in some countries, allow for working a limited number of hours per week. A BA course program is full-time and pretty intense, and jobs that students are able to obtain are usually not very well paid and are in retail or hospitality. One has to weigh the pros and cons of investing time in part-time work, when studying on a full-time course.

Internships

Internships are highly recommended. They can be paid or unpaid, one has to check regulations in the relevant country. Many designers start their careers with apprenticeships and internships. One can expect to be doing mundane and not very glamorous tasks, cutting fabrics, sewing toiles, sorting patterns and fabric rolls, dying swatches, and even making coffee etc. Nevertheless, internships offer a chance to be immersed in the atmosphere of a business and if lucky to meet legendary designers in person.

College can assist with internship placements, particularly if it is a part of a BA programme which includes one year in the industry experience.

Clientele

This may come across as an unusual paragraph in the "While in College" section, but the reality is, you need to make the most of your time to start accumulating potential clientele and future patrons of your talent. Those who would be eager to buy pieces from your graduation and future collections.

Clientele-Base Case Study: "While in college, a fellow student's mother was coming to town and hosting designer clothes Pop-Ups, which she was bringing from Italy, and asking everyone to attend and invite friends, which many of us did. By the end of the degree this particular student had a ready clientele list and went on to set up her own atelier. While others were not so lucky to have such a mother".

Graduation Show and Exhibition

By this point, one is usually exhausted, but it is the time to shine. A good school usually works hard to invite people from the industry to see your work. It is a chance to get noticed, get employed, get into the press, and get on the radar of the industry. Your classmates will also remember you for your graduation collection and your personality during these stressful times.

Some of the challenges students approaching graduation face, are pressure and stress over the perfection they desire to achieve. Students may suddenly feel they are not coping with illustrations, or their pattern cutting is not as good as they would hope for. One can inquire with a specific school, but it is usually not prohibited to engage help on some part of the collection, as one would in real life. Fashion is team work. Befriending students from the Creative Pattern Cutting division, Photography and Promotion Courses in advance can be handy. One can use students from years below as helpers, and this is encouraged by the college, as they will have to go through the same experience soon.

The degree often culminates in a graduation fashion show and exhibition, where guests from the industry are invited. In St. Martins College, each year approximately 20 fashion graduates are chosen to participate in the Annual Fashion Show, at which the fashion industry, journalists, buyers, and celebrities are present. One can see personas like Madonna in the front row. This creates helpful exposure for the newly graduating talent, and for the college. At graduation shows, guests are given a tour through the room to look at your collection and sketchbooks. It is not unusual for press requests or job offers to follow. Make sure you have your name and contact details clearly visible on your portfolio, and business cards or QR code printed.

Give it Your Best Shot

Your wealth will be your acquired network, as well as your design skills, and the reputation of the college.

At the end of the degree, you may end up deciding that fashion is not an industry for you after all these years in college. Some fashion graduates to go on to become artists, or choose completely different professions. However, if you studied at a good college, this artistic training and experience will still benefit you in many ways.

Masters or no Masters

A significant percentage of St. Martins BA graduates head immediately, or after several years, into a postgraduate MA degree. As per my observation, MA graduates from my college have obtained higher positions, and in more prestigious brands, than BA graduates, but not necessarily. Graduates go on to set up their own labels, either after a BA degree or after an MA. A postgraduate degree obviously requires an additional investment of money and time, 1 to 2 years. Proceeding with further education usually depends on how one feels about their own readiness as a designer, and other circumstances and ecosystem. Stella McCartney launched her label fresh out of her BA degree, on the wave of the buzz garnered from her BA graduation show. Alexander McQueen launched his label after completing an MA, prior to which he was already a proficient tailor and had worked in fashion in Italy.

Conclusion

Education is a significant investment of money and time. A good fashion school gives an excellent framework for becoming a fashion designer, whether employed on a corporate ladder or setting up a fashion label. Studying in the right school can be the experience of a lifetime. Many designers succeeded in fashion design or fashion entrepreneurship without any formal education. However, it seems to be a requirement for practically any fashion position advertised, these days.

Chapter 5

Fashion Career

Fashion design is one of the most competitive careers to get into, particularly at the high-end. To get an idea of employment options and salaries, one can consult with the Careers Office at the College you are studying. Alternatively, research the current fashion jobs market on popular industry websites such as BOF (Business of Fashion).

Recently, we noticed a trend for full-time BA students to run a small business selling their own designs, or vintage, while studying at fashion college for a fashion degree. One can see booths of recent UAL graduates (of which both St. Martins and London College of Fashion LCF are a part of) exhibiting at London trade exhibitions, such as Top Drawer and London Fashion Week. It looks like this career is taking a more versatile and entrepreneurial shape.

Some students are lucky to get a job straight out of college, or even while still at college. A fellow student at St. Martins was snatched from the Women's Wear BA course, because Dior was urgently looking for someone to draw, of course in the style of Dior, and the course supervisor recommended him. But this is rather an exception than a rule.

Essentially, in fashion, one has two options: to be employed and make a career on the corporate ladder, or to take a risk and start one's own label.

Employment

Salary Expectations

It is important to know that a starting designer's salary, even at a very prestigious heritage brand, can be only 22,000 Euros per year in Paris and Milan. With more senior fashion design positions in the USA paying around 150,000-200,000 dollars per year. The sky is the limit if you are an entrepreneurially inclined designer, like Tom Ford, who recently announced to the press he is a billionaire after Estee Lauder, the cosmetics giant, acquired his brand. The incredibly financially successful Michael Kors empire has recently acquired Versace.

Current salaries in fashion can be checked on the recruitment sites such as Business of Fashion, Drapers, LinkedIn Jobs, etc.

Search Routes

In a job search, one usually optimises every possible route. It is particularly good to look for work when one is hot out of a college graduation show, has some press coverage, or has just won a design award. A lot of talent scouting in fashion is done through word of mouth.

College Careers Office

Every respectable college has a Careers Office, which can offer guidance. In my college it was a window to which I came occasionally, to ask if there were any openings, but there were rarely any. Course directors and tutors were more likely to be helpful, as they often maintained relationships with their former students who had gone on to work for fashion houses or had started their own brands, and were now looking for talent to employ. Louise Wilson was a legendary MA course director at St. Martins who placed many of her graduates with top fashion brands.

Direct Applications

In the modern digital age, most houses and fashion groups have a jobs section on their website, where positions are listed and one can apply online directly to their Human Resources managers.

Online Platforms

The following platforms are a valuable source of information on current jobs available and their requirements:

LinkedIn Jobs
Drapers Jobs
Business of Fashion BOF
Eyes On Talents
Le Book

Headhunters

Headhunter agencies are likely to come to you when they have already heard of you and your talent, rather than you going to them. Examples of these agencies are, the renowned Denza in the UK and Agent Secret in France, which are overwhelmed with applications, considering how many fashion graduates there are in the world each year.

Work Application Requirements

CV. Should include an up-to-date list of education, work experience (paid and unpaid), other skills, such as computer programs and languages. Awards and nominations, if such are present. Contact details etc.

Cover Letter. This should describe why you are fit for this position company, and demonstrate knowledge about the company you are applying to and its ethos.

Portfolio and Digital Mini-Portfolio. Perspective employers need to see your style, as well as the creative thinking process behind your work, and how it suits their brand identity. A physical portfolio usually comes in a format of a folio book with sleeves, and includes visuals of designs and demonstration of processes behind it, showing an authentic research and development leading to final designs. If you have sketchbooks which are particularly beautiful you should bring them, or the best extracts, to interviews. When applying online, one attaches a smaller digital version of a portfolio.

Recommendations. Usually from two credible people, who know you and have worked with you. It may be someone from college if you have not been employed yet.

Barriers

It requires money and effort for an employer to obtain a work permit for someone who is not a citizen. Depending on the country regulations and procedures vary.

Opportunities

Despite being such a competitive industry, fashion has some unique opportunities, which we unveil in this book. Progressive individuals and organisations are interested in supporting creative talent, and in making grants and competitions available.

Internships and Assisting

Internships in fashion are a long-standing tradition. Recent regulations in some countries require at least minimal payment. Either fashion schools can arrange internships for their students, particularly as part of their course programme or one can send inquiries directly to their favourite brands.

Olivier Rousteing started with an internship at Roberto Cavalli prior to becoming a designer for his lines, and later moving on to take the helm at Balmain in 2011. Many famous designers started as apprentices.

Internship Case Study: "I had internships as a part of my BA course. I was lucky to find them in the studios of Alexander McQueen and Vivienne Westwood and to interact with both of these legends. Such experience made the possibility of setting up my own label more real to me".

Fashion Design Competitions and Festivals

"Without culture, and the relative freedom it implies, society, even when perfect, is but a jungle. This is why any authentic creation is a gift to the future"

-Albert Camus-

If one was not in an international college, and press and industry did not come to the final show, fashion design competitions are a great way to obtain the support and exposure one deserves.

Competitions are one of the best ways to get noticed, sometimes to launch one's whole career. Winners and runners-up increase their chances for employment, investment offers, and exposure to creative industries and to a broader public. Collections entering competitions should be very strong and demonstrate a level of acceptance in the industry already. Some competitions accept designers from their territories only, while others accept applicants from worldwide. Some of the most famous and respected fashion competitions are:

LVMH Prize for Young Fashion Designers (France). Open to designers from all over the world, aged 18 to 40, who have created at least two womenswear, menswear or genderless collections.

Kering Generation Prize (China, Japan, Saudi Arabia). A competition designed to discover and support innovative start-ups making a meaningful impact on sustainability within the fashion industry.

The Hyères Festival (France) promotes young artists in the fields of fashion, photography and fashion accessories. Each year, the festival organises three competitions as well as exhibitions, conferences and panels, in the town of Hyères and specifically at villa Noailles.

ITS (Italy) International Talent Support Contest, is a prestigious international award open to emerging fashion, accessory, and jewellery designers.

The International Woolmark Prize (Australia). Originally founded as International Wool Secretariat in 1936 to promote wool to the global market. It counts Valentino, Yves St. Laurent, Karl Lagerfeld as past recipients, when they were young up-and-coming designers.

NewGen (United Kingdom), short for New Generation by BFC British Fashion Council, has been going for decades and has supported multiple designers with funds, showcase, catwalk and business advice. Winners and recipients include Mary Katranzou, David Koma, Masha Popova, to count a few.

CFDA/Vogue Fashion Fund (USA) was established to help emerging designers and cultivate the next generation of American fashion talent.

It is recommended to keep an eye on relevant fashion organisations in one's own country, as well as internationally. Existing prizes and grants can be changed and new ones can be added. More progressive governments tend to care about their new and established talents, because they play an important part in maintaining and progressing a countrie's culture and heritage.

Designer Awards Case Study: "As a recent St. Martins graduate I was already trading, starting with my graduation collection samples. I saw some of my classmates in the press, winning awards such as New Gen, but had no clue how they did it. I was already overwhelmed enough, designing and interacting with customers who were mostly friends. Besides, I believed my womenswear collections were not big enough anymore, as I reduced them to the minimum of what I was sure customers would buy. At that time, I was taken with my new product – scarves – which I invented by draping fabrics I had originally designed for my womenswear. I decided to check the British Fashion Council website, where to my surprise, I discovered not only the NewGen competition, which required full womenswear collections, but the new competition titled "New Talent Launch-Pad Award" in collaboration with Elle magazine, which had an Accessories category. I filled in an application online. Luckily I already had retailers and all the requirements matched. When I went to meet the round table of judges, and they started saying how much they love my prints and how unique they are, my voice was trembling. I received a call that I was one of the winners, and it was one of the happiest and most encouraging events a new designer can experience".

Chapter 6

Fashion Career

Own Brand

Launching one's own brand is the culmination of every designer's career, it entails the freedom of creative self-expression designer usually crave. In terms of how much money a fashion business can make – the sky is the limit. Tom Ford, who launched his eponymous label as recently as 2005, announced his billionaire status after selling his fashion brand to Estée Lauder in 2023 for a reported $2.8 billion (Forbes).

The richest designer in the world is Italian Giorgio Armani. After co-founding fashion retailer Giorgio Armani S.p.A. back in 1975, he became one of the richest people in the world today, coming in at an impressive number 135 at the time of writing (Forbes). The Milan-based fashion retailer's in-house distribution network has over 2,980 points of sales in 46 countries (Bloomberg), with brands including Armani Exchange, Armani Jeans and Emporio Armani. While most of Armani's fortune is derived from his ownership of Giorgio Armani S.p.A., he increased his net worth by launching Armani Hotels & Resorts in 2005.

It takes a lot of effort and exceptional marketing to reach and maintain a sufficient turnover for a new designer. Fashion is a strenuous and fast-changing industry, and one has to sustain the success rate by retaining the same customers while acquiring new ones, at the same time producing extremely desirable collections each season. Making a "weak" collection design-wise can lead to a loss of customers and decrease of cashflow in that season. Fashion designers have to be prepared to survive through economic challenges and de-stabilising world events, such as Covid which kept stores closed for a long time; or losing regular distribution territories to wars, and other factors.

Changing Business Models

Classic Wholesale Model

In the 1980-90s many fashion graduates went on to set up their own labels using a relatively simple business model: a good designer was creating a collection, usually with the help of a small team, and had a PR and a Sales Showroom. Sometimes, a fashion designer held a fashion show. Press wrote about the collection, and if a it was good press, stores came to the showroom and placed wholesale orders. Orders were manufactured and delivered to shops. When a retailer placed an order, it usually carried on buying from the same designer for many seasons, because it had to build-up and maintain clientele dedicated to this designer. This was pre-internet, and it was not easy for stores to find designers which suited their style and clientele, as they had to travel afar to see collections and to get a sense of quality, materials etc. Look Books and Line Sheets were printed on paper and mailed by post. Orders and checks also had to be mailed by post in those days.

If a designer signed many orders and received distribution deals, the business became a big brand. Small and medium designers were exhibiting at the same tradeshows for decades, meeting their regular stores' customers from year to year, and building long-standing friendly relationships.

Designer Case Study: "I remember those days of meeting regular customers and fellow designers from year to year at "our" tradeshow in Paris - Premiere Classe, many of whom became very warm acquaintances. I caught this vibe in 2011-2015, before the internet changed retail so much. I sometimes miss it".

New Business Models

The situation in fashion and retail began to change in the 2000s, and more drastically from 2015 onwards, with the further expansion of internet shopping and social media. It became more viable for stores to buy designers who are "trending" and drive attention to a store, than the other way around. Look Books started being sent by e-mail, bombarding buyers, and stores did not have as much need to commit to the same designers. It became easy to swap from one to another, depending on press and social media trends.

Online shopping continued taking more and more market share. A lot of physical retail went into decline, with some renowned boutiques, such as Colette in Paris, closing down. While some retail models were phased out, new opportunities were opening associated with online sales and influencing.

The "classic model" of wholesaling to stores is still working but only to some degree. New and independent designers are increasingly turning to a direct-to-consumer model. With platforms such as Instagram and TikTok Shopping one can communicate directly to consumers and build relationships with audiences. Building and maintaining a pool of customers is a challenging and expensive task, but it is rewarding as the designer can keep all of the margin, instead of selling through intermediaries (retailers).

It is an increasingly popular trend for fashion design students to have a "side hustle" selling their creations during studies, on platforms such as Depop etc. and beginning to build their own audience. One can argue that juggling these sales activities can take focus away from the designer's training. It depends if a student wishes to take the more creative or the more entrepreneurial path after graduation.

Advertising and marketing industries have changed tremendously. Modern advertising gravitates towards online giants, Google, Facebook, and the likes. Also, towards the same platforms where brands retail, such as TikTok, Amazon etc.

Traditional media, such as print (publications on paper, magazines and newspaper supplements), TV, billboards — has declined in usage.

Social Media now plays a major role in promoting a designer and their brand. It is recommended to identify the most suitable and effective channel for a brand, and focus on that channel.

Public Relations is also changing with a bias for online versus print. Seasoned PR specialists and agencies are adjusting to these new trends.

One can say the concept of "marketing mix", a combination of different medias, is still relevant, but there are more digital and fast-changing components.

Fashion Accessories

In terms of business, producing accessories is slightly less complicated than clothing, as there is no need for fitting, or to produce various sizes as with clothing, and for this reason there are fewer overstock problems. Accessories are slightly easier to store and transport, versus whole womenswear or menswear collections. In shoes, business is complex and varied sizing is a nightmare, as it is in clothing and lingerie.

Partnerships

Statistically, designer partnerships and designer duos are more likely to survive than a solo designer. This is likely due to more mutual motivation to stay on track through challenging situations in this business. Some partnerships end up not getting on, literally pulling each other's hair out, and they part ways.

What Takes So Much Money?

A designer fashion business requires both outstanding creative output, and high business and management standards, to succeed. Creating and building a fashion brand is a capital-consuming endeavour. It is not widely known, but it can take 20 million pounds or more, to get a new luxury fashion brand off the ground. This usually takes several stages of financing and re-acquisition, for a brand to reach a break-even point. In accounting, BEP (breakeven point) is the production level at which total revenues equal total expense.

This may sound like crazy sums of money in the world of small business, but the scale is not unusual in the world of venture capital and finance, where brand valuations reach hundreds of millions and even billions. It is good to be aware of the venture capital and financial side of fashion and luxury business sooner rather than later. One would have to write a different book to get into this subject.

Setting it All Up

Setting up a company is not difficult or expensive, one can do it oneself with several hundred dollars and help from an accountant, and start trading. Unless you decide to go big from the start and use expensive services to advise and execute aspects such as:

- More complex company incorporation, for example an international entity.
- Worldwide trademarking.
- Brand DNA formation done by a large expensive agency, which caters to big companies.
- Employing a global PR agency on a large monthly retainer, from the start.
- Hold a massive launch event and campaign.

Research & Development

Designer Fashion, aka Premium Fashion, is all about R&D. Every season, or even more frequently, one has to develop a new, distinct and desirable fashion collection: designs, concepts, patterns and more. It is not the same as selling the same pair of leggings in different colours every season. Innovative designer collections require many hours of labour. This involves in-depth creative research, pattern-cutting, sampling, and all parts of a creative cycle. It is tough and exhausting work to create so much novelty to such a high standard, as in premium fashion. In the UK, fashion R&D does not qualify to claim tax credits, as it is not considered technologically innovative.

USP

Unique Selling Proposition involves a learning curve. A brand can go for several seasons until it's USP "stabilises". This can be through trial and error. Sometimes you think some idea, audience, business model, or point of differentiation is what will make your label sell. Often it is something unexpected that becomes your most successful design, or most lucrative market.

Rent

Designer fashion is a space-consuming practice because of its original creative development processes. It requires space for pattern-cutting on large tables, fittings, storing of fabrics and visual references for future collections etc. Samples have to be shown to customers, and stock needs to be stored and shipped from somewhere. It is not a virtual business that can be done exclusively from a laptop. On top of strenuous artistic work, a designer has to remain sociable: to give interviews, spend time with customers and industry – and so renting a work space far out of town is not a solution. Premium fashion thrives on organic relationships with people and appropriate spaces. Rent is a difficult expense, as it practically consumes every profit a designer begins to make, instead of reinvesting it back into business and marketing. So, it is not unusual to see young designers, even those who already hit a million dollars sales benchmark, being based in a part-subsidised location for creatives.

Marketing and Advertising

Designer fashion is not a "first necessity" product. The market is already saturated. New designers flourish only because they bring something distinct to the market and manage to grasp the spirit-of-the-time better than established designer brands. The difficult part is to engage those first several thousand customers, and to stay on their radar through advertising and PR. There is also an expense with tradeshows, to make oneself known to Business to Business (B2B) customers: stores and distributors. Marketing, advertising and PR are major expenses for a new fashion business, and not something to economise on.

Margins

Like most industries, fashion is subject to "economies of scale" i.e., the more you produce, the less is the cost of production and the more margin you retain. New fashion designers most often have no choice but to go on for a while with small margins, until the brand becomes more established with bigger distribution and production volume.

Designer Key Business Models

A designer has the biggest margins when selling Direct-to-Consumer (D2C), such as through their own e-commerce or their own shops. D2C brands can make a 2-6 times mark-up, depending on the cost of production and relevancy to the market. In other words, something that costs 100 dollars to make can be priced at 200-600 dollars on a shop floor. The challenge is the new Customer Acquisition Cost (CAC). The seemingly high mark-up of D2C model all gets consumed by the costs of advertising & marketing. It is expensive and challenging to attract customers to a new name in fashion, and to make them buy from online or physical stores. For new brands, margin can be negative for a while, until a designer reaches better economies of scale with higher margins. The key is to build up a list of regular customers who are making repeat purchases.

If a designer retails D2C through their own stores, this seemingly large profit margin gets eaten up by the cost of marketing, rent, staff salaries, taxes etc.

When a designer wholesales to retailers (boutiques, department stores), it is a Business-to-Business (B2B) model. A designer usually makes as little as 2 times mark-up. Meaning something which was made for 100 dollars, would wholesale at only about 200, or even less. Retailers make their own 2-

3.5 times mark-up, making the product price in retail approximately 600. Retailers also struggle and already have regular customers and traffic to their locations. They make such significant mark-ups to cover huge expenses on building rent, staff, returns handling etc.

As one can see, selling D2C or B2B both have their own advantages.

Wholesale model (B2B):

- May suit a designer who is design-focused and for whom it is too much to deal with individual customers in multiple small transactions and returns.
- Retailer orders a collection, pays a deposit. No need to finance and keep stock.
- Stores are cautious to order from new designers, due to concerns of receiving products of worse quality than samples, and in time. It becomes easier to be taken on by agents and retailers if you have proven yourself by already having successfully sold to a few stores.
- Margins for a designer are insignificant, retailer makes a large mark-up.
- Dangers of retailers delaying payments, or having unrealistic for new designers terms.

- High cost of tradeshows and showrooms where retailers can be reached.
- Intermediaries, agents and distributors, take an additional 10-25% commission on wholesale orders they have generated for a designer.
- A designer does not obtain final contact with customers and cannot retarget those who bought their products in stores.

Direct to Consumer (D2C):

- Great Margin
- Owning customers contacts/databases with opportunity re-target.
- Large investment into marketing towards building-up one's own audiences and maintaining them.
- Being a designer and retailer all-in-one. Dealing with many small transactions and returns. Artistic quality can start to suffer.
- Need for financing and keeping stock.
- Dealing with unsold stock.

Stock Financing

It is unlikely that a fashion manufacturer will give credit to any new designer, they will want you to pay a deposit to begin production, and pay the rest of the balance when goods are ready to ship. This can be a lump sum payment, even before you begin to sell these goods. Some banks can provide "order financing" (factoring) if you have a signed order from a well-known, reliable store.

Outsourcing Design

White label is a type of service, where a manufacturer's team designs collections, and you can choose the items you want, put your own label and market and sell as your own collection. The disadvantage is that designs may not be original or exclusive to you.

Private Label. A company does everything for you from collection design and sampling, to production, while you still have significant input in design and development.

The above options are most often used by those who want to start a fashion business, but their strength lies elsewhere. For example, social media influencers. One of the reasons why influencers become designers and start their own labels, is because they are approached by manufacturers themselves seeking this partnership. Manufacturers are looking for someone with established audiences, who can potentially shop their fashion merchandise.

Usually, only highly original "designer" collections are able to accumulate that premium brand value, which would make them attractive for future brand acquisition.

Learning Curve

A common scenario we see happening when someone decides to be a fashion designer would be a girl who has the means to buy a Birkin bag, and decides to "invest" it in launching her own fashion label instead. The girl usually pays someone, a tailor or a sampling unit, to make several samples to realise her vision. The girl invites girlfriends and family to see this collection. She goes to participate in a couple of local pop-ups. After selling one item in several months, and not placing any wholesale orders, for obvious reasons, the girl gives up.

Usual Mistakes New Designers Make

- Not understanding demand on the market, own USP, audiences and strategy.
- Not networking with VC (Venture Capital) and business people early enough.
- Lacking knowledge about finance and accounting.
- Doing everything oneself, resulting in burnout.

Good Things for a Creative to Do Early On

- Have an idea of potential audiences, what one has got to offer in terms of USP. What one wants to achieve in terms of sales, growth, and exit plan.
- Know, or have someone who knows, about accounting, finance and venture capital.
- Learn and develop team-building skills.

Conclusion

Launching one's own fashion label makes sense if a designer feels there is enough energy, training, finances, favourable factors within the eco system, and has enormous drive and passion. Many families realize that for their artistic son or daughter to create is their whole life.

There is a certain flair to having one's own fashion label. It can be a lifetime endeavour, remembered by your children and grandchildren.

There are multiple success stories of fashion designers becoming a high-turnover business and reaching billion-dollar brand valuations.

Chapter 7

Ethical and Sustainable Fashion

Ecology and sustainability are pressing topics in relation to fashion in recent years. "Fashion and it's supply chain are the third largest polluting industry after food and construction" (according to NRDC, National Resources Defence Council, USA). The modern system of manufacturing and the promotion of fast, disposable fashion puts pressure on non-renewable and threatened resources, especially water, and produces vast quantities of waste and pollution.

Many great designers are turning to circularity and sustainability. The work of British designer, Christopher Raeburn, who pioneered the reworking of surplus fabrics and garments, such as de-commissioned military stock, into distinct and functional pieces, is found in some of the best stores around the world. Bottletop brand bags are stocked by prestigious retailers, such as Selfridges, and are thriving with their recycling and social campaigns strategy. The label By Walid, uses antique textiles to create unique premium-priced fashion garments and homeware. To count a few of those designers who made sustainability a part of their ethos.

According to Forbes: "the vast majority of Generation Z shoppers prefer to buy sustainable brands, and they are most willing to spend 10 percent more on sustainable products. The report also found that Generation Z along with Millennials are the most likely to make purchase decisions based on values and principles (personal, social, and environmental)".

With this increased interest in more sustainable, organic, biodegradable and recycled materials to be used in fashion and accessories; ethics, sustainability and ecology can and should become integral and powerful parts of a designer's marketing strategy.

Designer Sustainability Case Study: "Following training at the Centre for Sustainable Fashion, we increasingly started using Modal fabric. This yarn, made from beech trees, does not consume as much water as cotton or wool, doesn't contain synthetic petroleum-based materials, and so it won't shed microplastics when you wear or wash it. It is completely biodegradable".

What is Sustainability?

Sustainability is an approach which promotes environmental sustainability and social responsibility in any and every aspect of the fashion industry: design, production, frequency of collections, communication, use, end of life, etc. Circularity, durability, transparency and traceability are the foundations of sustainable fashion, which concern both manufacturers and consumers. Sustainable fashion can be defined in various ways, depending on the criteria taken into account.

- Eco-friendly — fashion associated with practices that are less harmful to the environment than conventional practices.

- Slow fashion — considers processes and resources required in production and values respect for the environment, animals and workers. The opposite of fast fashion, slow fashion advocates the purchase of better-quality clothes which will last longer, values diversity and integrity, and demands transparency across the value chain.

- Ethical fashion — takes into account the social (respect for International Labour Organisation conventions) and environmental context of production.

Increasingly, it is required by government organisations that one must be able to support these claims if promoted to consumers.

Sustainability in Premium Fashion

Premium and luxury fashion tend to be of very high quality and not dependent on trends, naturally giving it sustainability advantages: high longevity and high number of uses in wear, attractiveness for circularity. Bags and clothes by Chanel, Hermes, LV etc. are incredibly high in demand for upcycling.

Upcycling and luxury recycling retail is trending online and offline.

Sustainability Organisations and Education

There is a whole array of organisations supporting and promoting sustainable fashion, as well as universities offering Fashion Sustainability education.

The Centre for Sustainable Fashion is a research, education and knowledge exchange centre, based at the London College of Fashion.

Paris Good Fashion is a French organisation, which aims to accelerate the sustainable transition of the fashion industry. Besides everything else, its website has a great glossary of sustainability terms.

The United Nations Alliance for Sustainable Fashion is an initiative of United Nations agencies and allied organizations designed to contribute to the Sustainable Development Goals through coordinated action in the fashion sector.

Oxfam offers a Sustainability Education Guide for Teachers, with information, activities and ideas for learning about the impact of fast fashion.

London College of Fashion, with the support from Kering, offers "Fashion and Sustainability: Understanding Luxury Fashion in a Changing World" — a six-week course where you'll delve into sustainable fashion design, research, and business practice.

St. Martins College of Art and Design offers online Sustainability courses, such as "Communicating Sustainability in Fashion", "Sustainable Sourcing for Fashion" etc.

And the number of such organisations is growing, in an attempt to make the planet a saner place.

Vegan and Cruelty-Free Fashion

There is a growing demand for cruelty-free fashion, which can be sustainable, but it's not a guarantee. While avoiding animal products like fur, leather, wool, and silk reduces harm to animals and also the environmental harm associated with animal agriculture, some vegan alternatives like synthetic fabrics and leather substitutes can also have negative environmental impacts. The sustainability of cruelty-free fashion depends on the specific materials, production processes, and supply chain processes used.

Chapter 8

Practical Guidelines

How to Set Up a Label

If you have absolutely decided to conquer the fashion world then nothing can stop you setting up your own label.

It would be good if you already have at least one retailer who wants to stock your collection, and have several private clients who rave about your designs. And some financing.

Team

Anyone who has created a final collection at fashion college, already knows what they need people-wise and resources-wise to create a full marketable fashion collection. Roles can be permanent, or most often with small designers, seasonal and freelance. A minimal designer team most often consists of:

- A designer, who designs collections and stays true to their vision.
- A pattern cutter, can be freelance.

- A seamstress, can be freelance.
- A PR (Public Relations) who communicates with everyone and distributes information to press, making collections known and desirable. PR can also handle social media and customer relationships, for now.
- A sales person, someone who knows buyers and stores, and how to sell to them. It can be someone in-house, or a team in an external seasonal showroom.
- An accountant, usually external at this point.

Some designers can do all of these roles themselves, but in this case one is very likely to get burned out.

If you are an E-commerce focused designer, someone would inevitably have to handle online marketing and advertising:

- An in-house ads manager or an external online advertising agency.

Some of the other roles in a new designer studio can be:

- A studio manager, who takes care of the studio's day to day activities
- A production manager, someone who deals with orders, production execution and delivery.

- A CEO (Chief Executive Officer) of the business, who knows how to run the business, develop and execute strategy, do business development, manage fundraising, and handle investor relations.
- In-house accountant or CFO (Chief Financial Officer).

Begin to think about people who could eventually take these roles, as you progress.

Fashion Collection

For retail stores, a collection should be a minimum of 12 looks: coordinated tops and bottoms, full length one-pieces etc. Multi-brand boutiques can order a whole collection if they are in love with it and if it really suits their clientele. More usually boutiques order only select pieces, to mix and match with other brands in the store. For example, it is only a particular type of skirt or dress which may appeal to a buyer. Orders from boutiques can be as few as 5 pieces for a small designer, which you may agree to take or not, as it may not be viable to produce. For big stores, who have to fill at least one rail with one brand on the shop floor, a designer collection must be at least 20-30 looks. More realistically, for collections to be bought by department stores, we are talking about 100s of looks by the same brand, as you can see presented by serious showrooms and distributors.

Orders on womenswear designer collections can be in the range of $10,000 – 250,000. Brands set up order minimums to keep costs viable for production, but young designers who are desperate to be in retail may be less fussy and process even small orders.

It is for the individual designer to define at what scale to start, and at what pace they plan to progress financially and otherwise.

Accessories Collection

A collection should contain a sufficient number of pieces to present "a story", which would look good on display in a store or online. Occasionally, one comes across a stand at a tradeshow, which has a collection of only 5 bag designs and buyers are still buying it because it happens to be "in trend". A usual collection consists of many pieces and options to select from a number of colours and materials.

Business Entity

One can begin as a solo trader, but it is quite usual to register a business entity as an LLC or LTD early on. A good accountant can explain the differences, advantages and disadvantages, and register it for you quite inexpensively and quickly.

Accountants

There are some accountants who are more acquainted with fashion and retail than others, and this may be beneficial. It is also helpful to use online accounting platforms in which a designer can raise Invoices to customers, such as Xero, Sage or Quick Books. Inventory and Order Management systems like Bright Pearl include accounting in it.

Accountants and bookkeepers are not cheap, but a designer tends to need them, as creatives often can be easily over-whelmed by figures. A good accountant can save you a fortune in the long run.

Space

Everyone who completed a graduate collection knows how space-consuming fashion design is. A designer needs space for designing, sample making, stocking and shipping press samples, and taking appointments with select customers and friends of the brand.

Health and Safety

Fashion and textiles involve exposure to visible and invisible particles of dust and chemicals from the dyeing processes and other aspects of textile production, which can affect health. The pins, the needles and the machinery involved in fashion making are all hazards. It is not recommended to make fashion where one lives or sleeps.

Strategy and Business Plan

These words may sound completely new to an artist and a creative degree graduate, whose primary drive is to create, but one has to have at least some idea of who they are designing for and how to reach them. If a young designer is someone who loved running a TikTok account in college, this is probably the channel to continue developing. Or, if a designer is someone who won a design award from which he received store orders, this can be the type of strategy to carry on developing. Some business aspects can develop organically.

Organisations such as banks, funding and grants bodies, and of course, investors, will ask you for a Business Plan, often with figures and projections, to demonstrate to them how you are planning to grow your business. It is recommended to secure a friend, family member, or someone who is knowledgeable and can help with these aspects.

Branding

Brand building is an interesting discipline, which includes the creation of a brand identity. That which makes a brand distinctive, memorable and desirable to its audiences. Most designers are an original brand in themselves. There are specialist consultants and creative directors who can conceptualise a brand.

A Brand Name is often a designer's own name, or a specially selected name to reflect the brands concept and philosophy. Such as, Demna Gvasalia's Vetements brand, the French word meaning clothes; or Virgil Abloh's Off-White brand. Check the availability of trademark and domain names for the name you selected.

Have some brand identity foundations, to be used on the website and in communications. These can be developed by an agency, or by oneself:

- A logo.
- Selection of fonts to use across website and print.
- Brand colours, to use consistently in logo, packaging, and all aspects of brand identity.

Trademarking

It is not complicated to file a trademark registration oneself directly to an intellectual property office. You can use an online company like Trademarkia, or engage an intellectual property lawyer or a law firm.

Research whether a desired name is already taken, and identify trademark classes one wishes to secure.

Website and social media

Website and social media accounts are essential. They play a major role, especially if your brand has a direct-to-consumer strategy selling online.

You can have a website custom-made by a professional agency and developer. Many websites, even for the biggest brands, are designed on standardised platforms such as Shopify, Magento, Wix etc. Platforms provide free or affordable templates - it is easy to make a website oneself.

Secure a web domain relevant to the name you will be using, and social media extensions. Domains with .com extension are preferable, but we have seen designers using all sorts of domains successfully.

Visuals and Product Photography

Fashion designers need continuous content more than ever, for promotion and exposure in social media and press. The usual routes to create fashion collection photography are:

1) Outsourcing to a company specialising in fashion photography. The inconvenience is that one has to send a significant number of pieces at one time, as they cannot do only a few pieces, separately or additionally. Quality can be very professional, depending on the company. It is expensive.
2) Renting a photo studio to shoot visuals seasonally. Gives more creative control. Is limiting if you need to add photography continuously.
3) In-house photography, which takes space and requires expensive equipment. More and more designers tend to have some form of their own photography facility, due to a continuous need for content.

Investors

In the early stages your investors are very likely to be your own family, a partner, a father, someone you know and who loves your talent and believes in you. Maybe they do not even believe in you, but they realise you are an artist and creativity is your life. Fashion labels are rarely started with a small bank loan, as it is usually not something returning capital immediately.

Banking and Finances

Hardly any business can grow without the use of financial products and borrowing. A good starting point is to have a knowledgeable bank manager, who can guide a young brand through available banking products: loans, overdrafts and factoring financing (to cover cost of orders from reliable stores in advance). As a fashion brand grows it is likely to have a CFO (Chief Financial Officer).

A designer often carries a lot of financial risks. They would have to pay a deposit on production (30-40%), money will be locked in stock and returns, as well other multiple and unpredictable things going wrong. Stores, even the biggest ones, can severely delay payments. It can take a year from the time you paid a production deposit until a store finally pays you.

Marketing and PR

In fashion it is of foremost importance that there is someone driving desirability and demand to your brand, your collections, and your website. A designer, as an artist, can be deeply immersed in creation. Even the most spectacular collection may go unnoticed. Exposure does not just happen miraculously; it is hard work which needs to be done.

One must have Marketing and PR, either in-house or externally. It can be an individual on a salary in-house, or a freelancer, or an agency. The advantages of an agency are that it has a team of people with different skills: classic press relations, celebrity placements, social media, etc. An experienced freelance consultant is often the first publicity option for a new designer, to lay foundations of strategy and first points of exposure. PR must be consistently maintained.

Some of the world-renowned fashion PR agencies are Karla Otto, Communications Store, Purple, PRco and Townhouse Consultancy, to count a few. Although it may sound unattainable, these agencies could agree to take on a new designer if they see true talent and potential. PR is not cheap.

It is important to establish one's own relationships with journalists and press. This can be journalism or advertising student friends you met in college.

Distribution

To decide on the overall strategy of a fashion brand, one needs to choose a type of distribution:

- Direct to Consumer (D2C), meaning a designer sells directly to the consumer, through their own stores or e-commerce.

- Business to Business (B2B), meaning a designer sells to other businesses/stores, which then retail to customers.

- Mixed model, a combination of various B2B and D2C channels.

Once you have decided on the business model you can work out the specifics of the plan: partners, targets, and financing. Decide which tradeshows to attend, and which showrooms and retailers to approach.

Types of Retailers

Significant changes have been taking place in retail space, we have seen a shift of budgets and buying power towards online retail.

Types of retailers which buy designer fashion collections:

Boutiques are smaller retailers which sell fashionable clothes. These can be mono-brand, selling one label exclusively, or multi-brand selling various labels. A boutique buyer can be the owner themselves, or an employee. It is important not to underestimate the importance of small boutiques in fashion — some boutiques are influential taste makers in the industry. If a designer is present in "the right" boutique it is a significant stamp of approval for other retailers to follow.

Department Stores are large stores divided into departments which sell such products as clothing, shoes, jewellery, cosmetics, furniture, electronics, toys etc. Harrods is a famous luxury department store in the UK, its flagship in Knightsbridge is the largest in Europe, and it also has several beauty branches and 8 airport branches. American department stores are on a different magnitude of scale: Saks 5th Avenue operates approximately 100 locations in the United States. When a department store orders a designer collection, it is likely be for all branches, or at least several. Department store orders are significant and a big win for a designer. Since 2015 an increasing trend is that department stores do not buy new designers, but rent out concessions/spaces, which primarily only big brands can afford.

Online Stores are the new breed of large influential retailers, which operate exclusively, or almost exclusively online. Net-a-Porte, My Theresa, Style Bop etc. are prestigious retailers, orders from which can be worth hundreds of thousands. The problem arises if such a retailer offers 50/50 terms, where 50% is a standard "paid" order, and 50% is on SOR terms (Sale or Return). Meaning, if a part of the goods does not sell in the store, for whatever reason, it will be returned to a designer at the end of the season. I know of at least 2 independent designers who went out of business in this way, as they were overwhelmed by returns and did not know what to do with the stock. Some terms can be too tough for small designers who do not have their own retail outlets.

Platforms for new designers, such as Not Just a Label NJAL, Wolf & Badger and others. These platforms will feature designers' collections and charge a commission when sales occur. These platforms do not place orders with designers in the way retailers do.

Pop-Ups. Some designers make Pop-Ups a consistent channel of their sales, setting up small stalls in hotels, private houses or other venues, for one or several days, together with other designers or exclusively. The organisers of these events can be individuals, companies or designers, who you can contact and request to join in. Collective Pop-Ups charge a fee, and do not guarantee sales. Your brand has to fit the price point and the social group, as all participants are sharing guests and customers.

Once you have defined and listed the retailers to which your collection may appeal, you can consider participating in tradeshows which their buyers attend. And think of other channels to get noticed by these retailers.

Designer Case Study: "When Harvey Nichols ordered our collection it was for their Knightsbridge branch, as well as for online. We were so happy."

Fashion Weeks and Tradeshows

It would be a part of a fashion brand's strategy to define in which fashion weeks, tradeshows, and private showrooms to participate, and in what countries.

Participation in the London Fashion Week Exhibition can cost several thousand pounds. One should contact LFW week to find out the exact current costs and locations. It is important to know that buyers rarely write orders at fashion weeks, or at fashion show, but it is a way to get noticed. Participation may help to establish credibility, and get press and social media coverage. Buying teams mostly write orders at tradeshows and in showrooms. Buyers are extremely busy: they have thousands of collections to view, and orders should strictly fit into their strategies and calculations. It is not easy to pull buyers into an independent showroom, but they are more likely to come if a brand is receiving a lot of press and social media attention.

There are a number of fashion tradeshows which buyers attend, such as Tranoi in Paris, White in Milan, Coterie in NYC, and many others. Modem Online has a list of all the major tradeshows and showrooms in the world. The websites of tradeshows feature a list of participating brands, to help you understand if this tradeshow is a suitable environment for your collection. It can cost in the range of 4,000 to 25,000 per stand at a tradeshow, depending on how many square meters you book.

It is recommended to visit fashion weeks, tradeshows and showrooms — to identify the ones which resonate with your design work.

A Fashion Show

Although, putting on a fashion show sounds like a dream, one should think twice before doing it for a small brand, as it usually costs 5,000 to 100,000 for a small designer, but the sky is really the limit. There are special production companies who organise shows for fashion brands, in high fashion the renowned Bureau Betak organises shows for Dior and many others. Some of these shows made history in terms of beauty and impact. Small designers sometimes organise a show on a budget using friends, as models, make-up artists and stylists. The advantage of hosting a good show, is that it makes a brand look established, and generates impressive content i.e. catwalk photos and videos for dissemination in the press and social media. A fashion show is mostly necessary for fashion brands to support their vast retail networks, as well as their cosmetics and perfume licences. Buyers do not write orders at a fashion show, they visit a brand's showroom. A small brand may be better off with a good quality presentation in a showroom than a fashion show, at this stage.

When you have a fashion label you are likely to receive invitations to participate in private fashion shows that take place outside fashion weeks, Charity Galas as an example. You are unlikely to make money from these fashion shows. But some will ask a designer to pay to participate, whereas some will just be happy to have your collection to entertain their clientele, or for whatever other purpose their fashion show serves. These types of shows are likely to create problems, such as causing damage to garments or losing pieces in transportation. The best you can get out of it is an occasional private client if you do one-off designs. Young designers sometimes agree to these shows, because they are hungry for exposure and pictures.

Manufacturing and Suppliers

One has to produce orders in time and of top quality. Production can be rejected by a retailer if it is not of the same quality as the samples it was ordered from.

Small designers can produce small orders in-house with the same seamstresses who made their samples. It is more usual to delegate a small production to a local manufacturing unit. There are small manufacturing units even in big cities, such as London Sewing Services, or Nadia Alexander in Scotland.

As soon as production minimums increase, the usual choice is to manufacture using factories in countries like Italy, Spain, Portugal, or further afield in Asia where even higher minimums are required.

Local. When manufacturing locally you have more control, as you can visit and perform quality control before the production is shipped out. Do not expect state of the art equipment, but you can be lucky to work with good seamstresses.

Italy. Offering premium level fitting and technical expertise, at this time nothing compares to fashion made in Italy. Advantages of Italian manufacturing are a long-standing tradition of credit and trust, but not always of timing. Do not expect everyone to speak English, but you will certainly be appointed someone who does.

Asia. Manufacturers in China are sometimes technologically better equipped, these days, than anyone else, but tailoring and pattern-cutting do not have the same long-standing tradition as Italy. One can find the right manufacturer through a special sourcing agent, or by visiting trade fairs. Intermediary quality control and shipping agents are usually necessary, which incurs additional cost. Huge minimums for production are required.

It is usual to start producing locally, and to expand globally as one progresses. Often manufacturers approach designers themselves by noticing a collection online or at a trade fair.

Fabrics and trimmings

Even small designers love visiting Premiere Vision, the leading premium fabrics and trimmings tradefair, which takes place twice a year in the north of Paris. Even though mills require significant minimums, a designer sometimes can negotiate to buy smaller quantities, as everyone wants to build long-term relationships.

There are enormous textile fairs in China, such as Shenzhen Textiles fair, but the minimum order requirements are larger than Europe. As well as there being language and cultural differences that one may encounter. In addition, quality control agencies should usually be involved when ordering from Asia.

A designer can secure relationships with premium fabric suppliers locally. For example, Laurent Garigue is an upmarket fabrics supplier with a showroom in London.

How to Stay on Top of Fashion Trends

To keep an eye on the most desirable colours and trends of the season, some fashion brands buy trend books from trend prediction companies, such as WGSN, Peclers Paris and Pantone.

Production Systems

In the beginning one can accumulate orders in Excel, and as one grows there are specialist production systems such as Zedonk.

Selling Systems

Orders are still often accepted traditionally by e-mail. The new way to place orders is through digital wholesale technology, platforms such as Joor, Le New Black, NuOrder etc.

These B2B marketplaces promote a concept of virtual showrooms, the new way for buyers to connect with brands, view collections and place orders. These can be costly.

Packaging and Labels

Suppliers are easily found online. Known companies like Weavabel are based in the UK, but tend to produce in Asia.

Packaging Case Study: "At VASSILISA we continue to manufacture our scarves gift boxes in the UK, which is a rarity. It is a slightly old-fashioned company mostly specialising in archival packaging. Embossing and gold leaf are used. We always prefer local and family-run manufacturers".

Shipping

Shipping can be a nightmare in the beginning, when you are only beginning to learn about the nuances of paperwork and duties. While shipping giants such as DHL, UPS, DPD and Fedex have almost taken total control of the shipping market, their customer support is more difficult to reach than ever before. You could be more comfortable using a smaller niche shipper experienced in fashion, such as CSM Logistics in the UK.

Supporting Organisations

Most countries have organisations representing and supporting the fashion industry and its exports. Some are governmental organisations or are privately funded. In the UK there is the British Fashion Council (BFC), which runs London Fashion Week with grant programs for new talent, amongst some of its activities. Other organisations are the UK Fashion and Textiles Association (UKFT), which offers helpful business advice, for example on finding a tradeshow suitable for a specific brand, which can save a lot of time and money. The Department for International Trade organises export networking events, Trade Missions around the world, and runs an Export Training Academy.

It is highly recommended to join fashion related organisations in the country where a brand is based.

Creatives

Fashion creatives are a big part of a designer's life: photographers, models and journalists are likely to become friends and supporters. Some brands take less of a personal approach, and employ creatives through agencies, for their campaigns.

Mentors

When you are a talented designer, you naturally attract positive cooperation, sometimes from very powerful people. One can ask such a person to mentor you in business. Some organisations provide mentorship and business advice as part of their grants and prize programmes.

Next Stages

When designer collections impress journalists and retailers, the label begins to attract orders, press requests, collaboration inquiries, distribution leads, and possibly investment interest. It can also lead to receiving offers of employment or consulting. Healthy turnover growth and consistently strong design can lead to a brand's eventual acquisition by a large company. In the ideal world one should have an idea of exact sales targets and company growth strategy. As well as facing the concept of business exit, to draw some scenarios and steps, which could lead to positive outcomes.

Establishing your own label can be a lucrative endeavour and an exciting adventure. It can be an extremely strenuous activity mentally and financially, for which a creative mind may not be prepared or trained for, in a design college. If you consider all the aspects mentioned in this book, such as ensuring favourable talent factors and business support — you will have a much higher probability of succeeding and enjoying your own journey in fashion and in life.

Thing that will increase the value of your brand and what you have achieved:

- Positive trajectory in sales volume.
- Profits (not always expected in the beginning).
- Number of customers and repeat customers.
- Quality of design work, which could have a "seal of approval" by winning design competitions or receiving favourable revies by respected fashion editors.
- Team, the quality and reputation of people who work for you, or with you.
- Brand value: how many followers you have, prominent customers, prestige retail channels you are taken

on by, important ambassadors, or business mentors involved with you.

Chapter 9

Success Stories

There are many examples of great success stories in the world of fashion design and among those who launched their own labels. On the other side there are those who tried fashion and switched over to a completely different discipline.

St. Martins Graduate Case Study

"From my St. Martins' BA graduation year in London, alumni currently work as designers at Loewe, Lanvin, Marni, Versace, Vivienne Westwood, Alexander McQueen to count a few. Some went on to become successful photographers or artists, such as Rachel Garrard in New York.

Those who started their own labels did it immediately after a BA degree, or after additionally doing an MA. From my year alone those who launched their own labels and are regularly featured in the press are Mark Fast, David Koma, Emilia Wickstead and my own VASSILISA. Lotta Volkova became an influential stylist for super brands, such as Miu Miu.

The fellow student designer who I liked the most, was Christopher Kane. He became a well-known brand after college and his talents were later acquired by LVMH.

The highlight of my own career was receiving a talent award from the British Fashion Council and Elle magazine in 2011/12 with my beloved brand VASSILISA. This was a huge encouragement, and gave me a boost in press and retail."

It is not always easy to define success. If one knew the figures involved in terms of investment and profitability of many well-known fashion brands one would be stunned. There can be huge financial losses in the intermediary stages and brands may continue being acquired and re-acquired, until they reach profitability. Premium brand financing is more complex than someone who is not in the business of fashion or luxury Venture Capital business could ever imagine. In the last two decades, we have seen such great successes such as Alexander McQueen and Tom Ford reaching multibillion brand valuations.

The ultimate success for a designer is simply satisfaction from creation, and knowing that you may have brightened the day and brought moments of joy to thousands of people around the world with what you made

References

Books
Donna Karan "My Journey"
Diane Von Furstenberg "The woman I wanted to be"
Karl Lagerfeld "A line of Beauty"
Paul Smith "50th Anniversary Book"
Neri Karra "Fashion Entrepreneurship'

Illustration Books and Resources
Howard Tangye "Within"
FIDA Publishing "The Fible"
Vieva Books "Luxury Scarves Colouring and Design Book"

Films
"Dior and I" 2014
"L'Amour Fou" (Yves St.Laurent) 2010
"House of Gucci" 2021
"Beauty Queens: Este Lauder" 1988
"Beauty Queens: Elizabeth Arden" 1988
"Beauty Queens: Helena Rubenstein" 1988

Book Shops & Libraries
Serpentine Gallery Book Shop, London
St. Martins College Library and Shop, London
V&A Museum Library, London
Armani Libri Library, Milan
Metrograph Cinema and Shop, NYC

Explore All Our Books

www.Vieva.co.uk

@vieva_books

@vievabooks

Scan Me

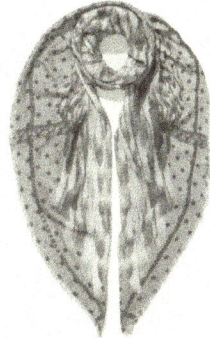

Notes

Notes